I KNOW WHAT TO DO! SOCIAL SKILLS

HOW TO RESPECT PERSONAL SPACE

CAITIE MCANENEY

PowerKiDS press.

Published in 2025 by The Rosen Publishing Group, Inc.
2544 Clinton Street, Buffalo, NY 14224

First Edition

Editor: Caitie McAneney
Book Design: Rachel Rising

Photo Credits: Cover, p. 1 SeventyFour/Shutterstock.com; pp. 4, 6, 8, 10, 12, 14, 16, 18, 19, 20 Cute art/Shutterstock.com; p. 5 Sergey Novikov/Shutterstock.com; p. 7 ORION PRODUCTION/Shutterstock.com; p. 9 Monkey Business Images/Shutterstock.com; p. 11 Dragana Gordic/Shutterstock.com; pp. 13, 21 Drazen Zigic/Shutterstock.com; p. 15 fizkes/Shuttestock.com; p. 17 Robert Kneschke/Shutterstock.com; p. 19 Anatoliy Karlyuk/Shutterstock.com.

Library of Congress Cataloging-in-Publication Data

Names: McAneney, Caitie, author.
Title: How to respect personal space / Caitie McAneney.
Description: Buffalo, NY : PowerKids Press, [2025] | Series: I know what to do! Social skills | Includes index.
Identifiers: LCCN 2024033148 (print) | LCCN 2024033149 (ebook) | ISBN 9781499450576 (lib. bdg.) | ISBN 9781499450569 (paperback) | ISBN 9781499450583 (ebook)
Subjects: LCSH: Personal space–Juvenile literature. | Interpersonal relations–Juvenile literature. | Social skills–Juvenile literature.
Classification: LCC HM1171 .M33 2025 (print) | LCC HM1171 (ebook) | DDC 158.2–dc23/eng/20240812
LC record available at https://lccn.loc.gov/2024033148
LC ebook record available at https://lccn.loc.gov/2024033149

Manufactured in the United States of America

CPSIA Compliance Information: Batch #CWPK25. For Further Information contact Rosen Publishing at 1-800-237-9932.

CONTENTS

What's Personal Space?

Imagine the space around your body as a bubble. That's your personal space. Your body and personal space belong to you. When others come in your bubble, it can feel uncomfortable. Respecting space is key to **communication**

Comfort Zone

Think of how it feels when you talk to someone. What makes you feel comfortable or safe? What makes you feel uncomfortable or unsafe? Think of your **comfort zone**. How far away do you want people to stand? Do you like to give hugs or high fives?

We're All Different!

Some people like to stand close to others. They might stand one foot away. Other people like to be farther from others. They might stand three feet away. Some people might like to hug and hold hands. Others may not like to be touched.

It Depends

Personal space **depends** on who is around you. You might love hugs from your mom. However, you may want more space from your classmates. You might stand close to your friends. You might stand far away from a new person.

Be Aware

People need to respect others' personal space and bodies. The first step is to be aware of your body. How close are you to others? Are you touching them or their belongings without **consent**? If someone says "no," always listen to them. No means no.

Looking for Clues

Are you in someone's personal space? Look for clues. If a person is comfortable, they will seem **relaxed**. They may look in your eyes or smile. If a person is uncomfortable, they may look away. They may be **tense** or look **nervous**.

Let's Practice

You can practice giving space. Have a parent or friend stand about a foot away from you. Talk with them. Do you feel comfortable? Do they look comfortable? If not, you can move farther or closer until it feels right for both of you.

Asking for Space

You **deserve** personal space, too. You are in control of your body. Notice how you feel around someone. If you need more space, step back. If the person is still too close, tell them. You can say, "Excuse me, I need some more space."

PRACTICE MAKES PROGRESS!

When you need personal space, you can say:

"I need some more space, please."

"Can you back up a little?"

"I don't want a hug right now."

"No. I don't want you to touch me."

All About Respect

When you respect someone, you treat their feelings and needs as important. You listen to their **boundaries**. They have a right to their comfort. Your actions let them know you care. Others deserve personal space. You deserve it too!

GLOSSARY

boundary: A limit to what someone is comfortable with.

comfort zone: Somewhere where someone feels at ease.

communication: Using words to convey ideas, thoughts, and feelings.

consent: Permission or approval.

depend: To be decided by.

deserve: To have a right to something.

nervous: Feeling worry or fear about something.

relaxed: Free of stress or worry.

tense: Feeling strained in body or mind.

FOR MORE INFORMATION

BOOKS

Emminizer, Theresa. *My Body Bubble*. Buffalo, NY: Enslow Publishing, 2024.

Hughes, Sloane. *My Body Is Mine: How to Give and Receive Consent*. Minneapolis, MN: Bearport Publishing Company, 2024.

WEBSITES

7 Activities That Help Kids Communicate with Others
www.pbs.org/parents/thrive/7-activities-that-help-kids-communicate-with-others
With a parent or teacher, explore activities that can help you learn communication skills.

How To Talk with Friends When You Have Autism
kidshealth.org/en/kids/autism-conversation.html
Personal space and communication can be harder for people who have autism. Check out this resource for tips on how to talk to people.

INDEX